Songs from the Heart

Worshipping GOD in Your Own Tune & Melody

Gerard Assey

Songs from the Heart: *Worshipping GOD in Your Own Tune & Melody*

By

Gerard Assey

Published by:
Gerard Assey
19/18, Palli Arasan Street
Anna Nagar East
Chennai - 600 102

ISBN: 978-81-979654-4-9

(Image courtesy: bedneyimages on Freepik- www.Freepik.com-Thank You)

Table of Contents

Preface

Worship is a deeply personal act of devotion, a love song to our Creator, and a pathway to intimacy with God. It's the quiet whispers of praise in solitude, the passionate outpouring of gratitude, and the moments when words fail, and only our hearts can speak. This book, **Songs from the Heart: *Worshipping GOD in Your Own Tune & Melody*,** is my heartfelt invitation to you—to explore the beauty of worshiping God with songs that emerge from the depths of your soul, offering Him something uniquely yours.

As I prepared this collection, I was moved by a profound truth: our personal worship brings God joy. In Scripture, we see this time and again, whether through David's spontaneous psalms, Mary's song of praise, or the glorious cries of angels in Revelation, "Worthy is the Lamb." Worship isn't bound by formality; it flows freely from a heart captivated by His glory. Each song here draws from the vastness of who God is—Creator, Savior, Redeemer—and from Scripture's rich tapestry, as well as our everyday encounters with His presence.

To deepen your experience, I've included ten heartfelt exhortations for each of the nine themes, which cover six songs each. These brief prompts invite you into deeper reflection and worship, helping to center your heart on the wonders of our Lord, from praising Him as the Creator of all to joining with angels in heaven's chorus. These exhortations are my prayer for you, to encourage you in reverent, joyful praise and to draw you closer to the heart of God.

This book is not about perfect melodies or flawless harmonies. It's about the sincerity of your praise and the desire to honor God with your unique voice. So, come as you are—soft or loud, structured or spontaneous—and let your worship rise as an offering.

May these songs bring you into His presence daily, reminding you that the God who created everything also delights in hearing your personal song of adoration.

In His grace and joy,

Tips for Using These 54 Songs to Worship GOD

Worship is more than just singing; it is an expression of the heart, a deep connection with God that transcends musical talent or structure. These 54 songs in this book are designed to give you the freedom to worship God in a way that is deeply personal to you. You don't need to be a professional musician or have a perfect voice to lift these songs to the Lord. They are meant to be sung with your own melodies, harmonies, and rhythms—making your worship experience unique and heartfelt.

Before each of the nine themes, you will find an exhortation that invites you to approach each set of songs with a specific heart posture. These ten exhortations provide spiritual guidance and insight to deepen your worship experience, aligning your spirit with God's character and His works. Let these brief, heartfelt messages stir your heart and open your soul to worship God in spirit and truth, encouraging you to sing with genuine passion, surrender, and joy.

This chapter will give you tips on how to approach these songs in a way that brings you closer to God, using your creativity and personal style of worship. Whether you are worshipping in the quietness of your home, in a group setting, or while going about your day, these tips will help guide you into meaningful moments of praise.

Embrace Your Unique Melody: Each of these 54 songs is written without a set tune, allowing you to create your own melodies. The beauty of this freedom is that it reflects the personal relationship you have with God. Your melody doesn't need to follow a professional structure—just let your voice flow naturally.

- ✓ *Start Simple:* If you are new to creating your own melody, start by singing the lyrics as if you were speaking to God. Use your natural voice inflections and tones. As you become more comfortable, you can experiment with longer notes or higher pitches.
- ✓ *Let the Mood Lead the Music:* Each song evokes a different aspect of God's character or work. For instance, a song about God's majesty as Creator may inspire a soaring, triumphant melody, while a song reflecting on Jesus' sacrifice may draw you to a quieter, more contemplative tune. Allow the emotions of the lyrics to shape how you sing.
- ✓ Example: If you're singing a song based on Revelation 4 where we join the elders and angels in praise, imagine the grandeur of that heavenly scene. Let your voice rise in awe and reverence, reflecting the splendor of that moment. In contrast, when singing about worshiping in Spirit and truth (John 4:23-24), your melody might be soft and introspective, as you connect with God in deep, quiet adoration.

Create Harmonies or Use Simple Instruments: If you're comfortable singing, you can create harmonies by layering your voice with different pitches. If you're in a group, invite others to sing with you and experiment with harmonies that resonate together. Harmonies add depth to the worship experience, allowing each voice to bring something unique to the overall sound.

- ✓ *Harmonizing with Simplicity:* If you're not familiar with harmonizing, keep it simple. Start by singing a song at different octaves, or try adding a single harmony note above or below your main melody.
- ✓ *Use Instruments Lightly:* You don't need a full band to accompany your worship. Simple instruments like a guitar, piano, or even a drum can provide a foundation for your melody. Play softly so that your voice and the meaning of the lyrics remain the focus. Use the instrument to maintain a rhythm or a chord progression that supports the flow of your melody.
- ✓ Example: In the song based on Psalm 150:6, where "everything that has breath" is called to praise God, you might want to add a steady rhythm with a drum or clap along, reinforcing the joyful energy of the praise. Alternatively, for the song reflecting Philippians 2:9-11, where every knee bows at the name of Jesus, a slow and reverent piano or guitar progression might fit the weight of the moment.

Worship in Different Environments and Times: These songs can be used for worship in a variety of settings. Whether you are alone, with family, or in a small group, these songs can become a part of your everyday worship routine. The flexibility of creating your own tunes allows you to adapt them to different moments.

- ✓ *Private Worship:* Use these songs in your quiet time with the Lord. Whether you're beginning your day or ending it, choose a song that reflects where your heart is and sing it as a personal prayer.
- ✓ Example: In the morning, you might sing a song about Jesus as Creator and Sustainer, reminding yourself that He is with you throughout the day. In the evening, a song about Jesus being your refuge and strength can help you reflect on His faithfulness as you rest.

Let the Lyrics Guide You into Deeper Worship: These lyrics were written with one purpose: to glorify God and draw you closer to Him. The words are simple yet profound, reminding us of God's attributes, His power, and His love. Allow the meaning of the lyrics to be the focus of your worship, using the melodies and harmonies you create to support and enhance the words.

- ✓ *Meditate on the Meaning:* Before you sing, take time to read through the lyrics and meditate on what they mean. Let each word resonate in your heart before you begin to sing. This can deepen your connection with the lyrics and make your worship more intentional.
- ✓ Example: In a song inspired by Philippians 2:9-11, reflect on the truth that "every knee will bow and every tongue confess that Jesus is Lord." Let that powerful truth shape your worship, leading you into awe and surrender.

Sing Spontaneously and Freely: Don't feel constrained by structure. One of the beautiful aspects of these songs is that they encourage you to sing spontaneously. You can sing the lyrics as they are written or add your own lines as the Holy Spirit leads. If you feel a sudden burst of praise or need to extend a song into more verses, follow that prompting. Worship is a dynamic exchange between you and God—don't be afraid to be free and expressive.

- ✓ *Spontaneous Worship Moments:* As you sing, you may find yourself adding words of thanks, personalizing the lyrics to reflect what God is doing in your life at that moment. This is spontaneous worship—a beautiful, raw expression of your love for God.
- ✓ Example: In the song based on 1 Chronicles 16:29, which speaks of giving God the glory due His name, you might spontaneously add your own praises, declaring specific ways God has worked in your life as you sing. This can turn a song into a longer, more intimate worship moment.

These 54 songs are not just words on a page; they are an invitation to explore and express your worship in ways that are unique to you. Let your voice be the instrument that carries these songs to the throne of God. Whether sung quietly in your personal time, with joyful noise in a group, or with spontaneous freedom in the moment, the goal is to glorify Jesus with all your heart. Let your worship be sincere, creative, and passionate as you offer up your own song to the King of Kings.

Part 1:
Praising HIM as the Creator and Master of Everything

Praising HIM as the Creator and Master of Everything

These exhortations serve as a powerful guide to encourage heartfelt and reverent worship, drawing you into deeper communion with the Lord. By focusing on the relevant them, they remind you of the awe-inspiring character of God and inspire a spirit of reverence.
These words help shift focus from daily distractions to God's greatness and goodness, creating an atmosphere of adoration and gratitude. They invite everyone to participate meaningfully, lifting hearts and voices with purpose and joy, and foster a space where worship becomes an authentic response to the divine, glorifying the Lord and drawing closer to Him.

1. *"Lift your voices to honor the One who spoke the heavens into existence and breathed life into all creation!"*
2. *"Today, let us stand in awe of our Creator, who made the earth, the stars, and the vastness of the universe by the power of His word."*
3. *"We worship the One who holds every mountain, every ocean, every soul in His hands—our Creator and Sustainer!"*
4. *"Come, let us marvel at the works of His hands, the beauty of creation, and the majesty of the heavens, for He is worthy!"*
5. *"Let our praises rise like the morning sun, honoring the God who formed us from the dust and knows every star by name."*

6. *"Our Creator's power is evident in the gentle breeze and mighty oceans. Let us praise Him as the true Master of everything."*
7. *"With grateful hearts, let's worship the One who fashioned the earth and filled it with His glory and wisdom."*
8. *"As we gather, remember that the same God who made the galaxies knows each one of us by name—what a loving Creator we serve!"*
9. *"Let all creation be silent as we lift our hearts, proclaiming our Creator's unmatched wisdom and infinite creativity!"*
10. *"Praise be to our God, the Alpha and Omega, who created all things and holds all things together. He alone is worthy!"*

Song: 1

Verse 1
You formed the earth, the stars, the skies,
With just Your word, creation flies,
The oceans bow at Your command,
The mountains rise at Your hand.

Verse 2
You spoke the sun and moon to shine,
All life responds to Your design,
The winds obey, the seas are still,
All things exist to do Your will.

Chorus
You are the Master of all creation,
We lift our voice in adoration.
All praise to You, the mighty King,
To You alone our worship we bring.

Verse 3
The creatures dance, the trees rejoice,
All of creation lifts its voice.
The earth proclaims Your majesty,
The heavens shout Your sovereignty.

Song: 2

Verse 1
You spoke the heavens into place,
The stars above reflect Your grace.
The earth beneath, the skies so wide,
All testify You are our guide.

Verse 2
The sun and moon proclaim Your might,
You formed the day, You shaped the night.
The seas resound, the mountains bow,
Creation sings to You right now.

Chorus
Creator, Lord of all we see,
We lift our praise and bend our knee.
Master of all, we sing Your name,
Forevermore, You stay the same.

Verse 3
The wind obeys, the trees rejoice,
All life responds to Your great voice.
Your hand upholds all things You made,
In awe and wonder, we're arrayed.

Song: 3

Verse 1
You stretched the heavens with Your hand,
The earth was formed at Your command.
The seas roar out, the mountains stand,
All life exists by Your great plan.

Verse 2
You spoke the stars into the sky,
Your power made the eagles fly.
The oceans deep, the rivers wide,
Declare Your name, forever high.

Chorus
Creator of all we see and know,
In worship, Lord, our hearts will bow.
Master of all, to You we sing,
Forever You are Lord and King.

Verse 3
From dawn to dusk, Your name is praised,
In awe, the heavens lift their gaze.
All things reflect Your mighty hand,
You are the Lord of sea and land.

Song: 4

Verse 1
You spoke the world with perfect might,
At Your command came day from night.
The stars align to sing Your praise,
The universe declares Your ways.

Verse 2
Mountains rise at Your decree,
The oceans bow in majesty.
Every creature in Your hand,
Reflects the work of Your great plan.

Chorus
Creator God, we lift Your name,
The Master of all things proclaimed.
We worship You, the Lord of all,
Before Your throne, we humbly fall.

Verse 3
You paint the skies in colors bright,
The heavens tell of endless light.
In every breath and every sound,
Your glory, Lord, is all around.

Song: 5

Verse 1
You set the stars in perfect place,
Your mighty hand sustains all space.
The earth declares Your wondrous might,
All nature sings of endless light.

Verse 2
The oceans bow beneath Your feet,
Each mountain whispers praise so sweet.
The heavens stretch at Your command,
Creator God, how great You stand.

Chorus
We praise You, Lord, Creator true,
The Master of all things You do.
In every work, in every sound,
Your majesty is all around.

Verse 3
The trees reach up to touch the sky,
The winds sing out Your name on high.
In all the world, Your love is found,
And in our hearts, Your grace abounds.

Song: 6

Verse 1
Before the world was formed, You stood,
In perfect power, in perfect good.
Through You, creation found its breath,
And life was born where there was death.

Verse 2
The stars proclaim Your wondrous light,
The heavens bow before Your might.
In every mountain, every sea,
Your hand of power we all see.

Chorus
Jesus, You are Lord of all,
At Your name, the mighty fall.
The Maker, Master, King of kings,
Creation lives, and nature sings.

Verse 3
The universe Your voice obeys,
It moves in rhythm with Your ways.
From morning dawn to twilight's hue,
Creation testifies of You.

Part 2:
Revelation 4:
Joining the Elders and Angels

Revelation 4:
Joining the Elders and Angels

These exhortations serve as a powerful guide to encourage heartfelt and reverent worship, drawing you into deeper communion with the Lord. By focusing on the relevant them, they remind you of the awe-inspiring character of God and inspire a spirit of reverence.

These words help shift focus from daily distractions to God's greatness and goodness, creating an atmosphere of adoration and gratitude. They invite everyone to participate meaningfully, lifting hearts and voices with purpose and joy, and foster a space where worship becomes an authentic response to the divine, glorifying the Lord and drawing closer to Him.

1. *"As the elders cast their crowns before the throne, let us lay our lives down in worship before our holy King."*
2. *"Today, we join the countless angels singing, 'Holy, holy, holy, is the Lord God Almighty, who was and is and is to come!'"*
3. *"Lift your hearts with the heavenly hosts, declaring the holiness of the One who sits on the throne forever and ever."*
4. *"As we worship, envision yourself before the throne, joining the elders and angels in endless praise!"*
5. *"Let us join the eternal chorus, lifting up the One who reigns in majesty and holds the universe in His hands."*
6. *"Our voices unite with the heavenly beings who worship ceaselessly, declaring the glory of our Lord and God!"*

7. *"Just as the angels and elders sing, let us lift up our songs with passion and reverence before His throne!"*
8. *"We are in awe of our holy God, whose glory fills the heavens. Join the angels in singing of His majesty!"*
9. *"He is enthroned above all creation, receiving endless praise. Let our worship rise as incense before Him."*

"Our praise joins the eternal worship of heaven, glorifying our King, who is surrounded by light and majesty."

Song: 1

Verse 1
Before Your throne, the angels sing,
With endless praise to You they cling.
The elders fall and cast their crowns,
Before the One in glory bound.

Verse 2
“Holy, holy,” the anthem cries,
To Him who reigns above the skies.
The creatures bow, the heavens roar,
In worship we forever soar.

Chorus
We join the elders, we join the host,
To praise the Father, Son, and Holy Ghost.
Worthy are You, O Lamb, we cry,
Be lifted high, O God Most High!

Verse 3
With every breath, our hearts proclaim,
The glory of Your holy name.
Forevermore, our voices raise,
To offer You eternal praise.

Song: 2

Verse 1
Before Your throne, we join the throng,
In endless worship, loud and strong.
The elders fall, the creatures sing,
To You, O Lord, our mighty King.

Verse 2
The angels cry "Holy" in praise,
In awe of You, their voices raise.
We bow before the heavenly host,
To worship You, O God, the most.

Chorus
We join the angels in the sky,
With endless praise, O Lord Most High.
Holy, Holy, we declare,
Your glory fills the earth and air.

Verse 3
The elders cast their crowns before,
The One who reigns forevermore.
With all of heaven, we unite,
To glorify Your endless light.

Song: 3

Verse 1
Around Your throne, the elders kneel,
In worship deep, their love is real.
The angels sing, their voices rise,
Declaring You, O Lord Most Wise.

Verse 2
They cry "Holy" night and day,
Before Your throne, they always stay.
The hosts of heaven lift their sound,
In awe of You, their praise is found.

Chorus
We join the song of heaven's throne,
To worship You, and You alone.
Holy, Holy, is Your name,
Forevermore You stay the same.

Verse 3
With golden crowns, the elders fall,
And worship You, the Lord of all.
With all of heaven, we adore,
And lift Your name forevermore.

Song: 4

Verse 1
The elders fall before Your throne,
With endless praise, to You alone.
The angels cry, "Holy is He,"
Your name resounds in majesty.

Verse 2
With every voice, we join the song,
To worship You, our God so strong.
The hosts of heaven lift their praise,
In endless awe of all Your ways.

Chorus
Holy, holy, is Your name,
The One who was, will ever reign.
We join with heaven, Lord, to sing,
To worship You, eternal King.

Verse 3
With crowns laid down, we bow before,
The One who lives forevermore.
Our hearts cry out, our voices soar,
In praise to You whom we adore

Song: 5

Verse 1
Around Your throne, the elders bow,
And all the angels worship now.
They cry aloud, "Holy is He,"
Your glory fills eternity.

Verse 2
With every sound, the heavens ring,
All creatures bow before their King.
Their voices rise in endless praise,
Proclaiming You for all their days.

Chorus
We join the chorus of the sky,
With angels' songs that never die.
"Holy, holy," we declare,
Your throne is high beyond compare.

Verse 3
With crowns laid down, we come to sing,
The praises of our Holy King.
The elders fall, the angels cry,
As all creation lifts You high.

Song: 6

Verse 1
The elders bow before Your throne,
And sing of You, the Holy One.
The angels cry aloud Your name,
And all of heaven does the same.

Verse 2
We join with those who sing Your praise,
With hearts and voices, hands we raise.
All heaven shouts, "Our Lord is King,"
Forevermore, we'll worship sing.

Chorus
Jesus, Lamb of God, so high,
We join the chorus of the sky.
With every creature, we declare,
Your endless reign, beyond compare.

Verse 3
In white-robed awe, we fall below,
And crown You King, Your glory shows.
With angel choirs, we raise our voice,
To worship You, our only choice.

Part 3:
Philippians 2:9-11:
Every Knee Shall Bow

Philippians 2:9-11: Every Knee Shall Bow

These exhortations serve as a powerful guide to encourage heartfelt and reverent worship, drawing you into deeper communion with the Lord. By focusing on the relevant them, they remind you of the awe-inspiring character of God and inspire a spirit of reverence.

These words help shift focus from daily distractions to God's greatness and goodness, creating an atmosphere of adoration and gratitude. They invite everyone to participate meaningfully, lifting hearts and voices with purpose and joy, and foster a space where worship becomes an authentic response to the divine, glorifying the Lord and drawing closer to Him.

1. *"Let us honor the name above every name, the name that causes every knee to bow and every tongue to confess!"*
2. *"We worship Jesus, who humbled Himself to the point of death, now exalted to the highest place forever."*
3. *"Bow before the Lord of all, for at His name every knee will bow, every heart will confess: Jesus is Lord!"*
4. *"Today, we surrender to the King of Kings, proclaiming that only His name is worthy of all honor."*
5. *"Lift up the name of Jesus, the name to which every nation, tribe, and tongue will one day bow!"*

6. *"In humble reverence, we come before the One whom heaven exalts and earth will one day honor."*
7. *"We declare Jesus as Lord of all! One day every heart will acknowledge Him, but today, we choose to praise!"*
8. *"At His name, all powers fall. Let us honor the One who reigns with unmatchable authority and grace."*
9. *"Let us bow our hearts in worship, confessing that Jesus alone is Lord over all creation."*
10. *"There is no higher name than Jesus. May we bow in awe and proclaim His name with every breath."*

Song: 1

Verse 1
At Your name, all knees will bend,
In heaven, on earth, it will extend.
No higher name, no greater throne,
All will confess that You alone.

Verse 2
The name of Jesus lifts the weak,
At Your command, all strength we seek.
The nations bow, the tongues declare,
Your reign is just, beyond compare.

Chorus
At the name of Jesus, we will bow,
In worship we surrender now.
No other name will ever reign,
Forever Yours, in joy or pain.

Verse 3
From east to west, from shore to shore,
Your name will be adored and more.
With hearts bowed low, our praise we bring,
You are our Savior, Lord, and King.

Song: 2

Verse 1
At Your name, the heavens shake,
All things must bow for Your name's sake.
No greater power, no higher throne,
All knees shall bend to You alone.

Verse 2
At Jesus' name, all chains will fall,
Your mighty name has conquered all.
In heaven and earth, we shout Your fame,
And glorify Your holy name.

Chorus
At the name of Jesus, every knee will bow,
In worship and surrender now.
No other name in earth or sky,
Forever lifted up on high.

Verse 3
From shore to shore, from age to age,
Your name resounds on every page.
With hearts laid low and voices raised,
We give You everlasting praise.

Song: 3

Verse 1
Your name above all names we sing,
At Jesus' name, all praises ring.
In heaven, on earth, and under the skies,
To You, O Lord, all knees shall rise.

Verse 2
At Jesus' name, all fear will cease,
Your name alone brings hope and peace.
In every tongue, Your name we speak,
For in Your name, the strong are weak.

Chorus
At Your name, every knee will fall,
In worship, Lord, You reign o'er all.
No higher name, no greater power,
We bow before You every hour.

Verse 3
The nations rise, their voices blend,
In honor of You, without end.
With every breath, we lift our praise,
To glorify Your mighty ways.

Song: 4

Verse 1
At Your great name, the nations bow,
Before Your throne, we worship now.
No higher name, no greater sound,
Than Jesus' name, forever crowned.

Verse 2
In every land, Your name we raise,
At Jesus' feet, we give our praise.
Above all names, You stand alone,
In worship, Lord, we make You known.

Chorus
At Your name, every knee will bend,
Every voice to You ascend.
In heaven and earth, we'll glorify,
The name of Jesus, lifted high.

Verse 3
The humble come, the mighty fall,
Before Your name, You rule them all.
With hearts bowed low, we lift our song,
And to Your name, we all belong.

Song: 5

Verse 1
At Your great name, all knees will bend,
To You, our worship will ascend.
No other name is high or true,
Only the name belonging to You.

Verse 2
On earth, below, in heaven high,
We lift Your name to glorify.
Jesus, the King who reigns above,
In awe we bow, proclaiming love.

Chorus
At the name of Jesus, we bow low,
The name by which all things must grow.
In every place, in every land,
Your name alone will ever stand.

Verse 3
We raise Your name in every song,
In worship, where we all belong.
With every voice and heart and hand,
We bow before Your great command.

Song: 6

Verse 1
At Jesus' name, all knees will bend,
His reign will never see an end.
Above all names, He takes His place,
And we are covered by His grace.

Verse 2
From heaven's throne to earth below,
Your name, O Jesus, we will know.
In every heart and every land,
All knees will bow at Your command.

Chorus
Jesus, name above all names,
You break the chains, You heal the pains.
In every heart, in every tongue,
Your name is sung, forever young.

Verse 3
The heavens shout, the earth replies,
At Your great name, we lift our eyes.
And in Your power, we proclaim,
The endless glory of Your name.

Part 4:
Psalm 150:6:
Let Everything that Has Breath Praise the Lord

Psalm 150:6: Let Everything that Has Breath Praise the Lord

These exhortations serve as a powerful guide to encourage heartfelt and reverent worship, drawing you into deeper communion with the Lord. By focusing on the relevant them, they remind you of the awe-inspiring character of God and inspire a spirit of reverence.

These words help shift focus from daily distractions to God's greatness and goodness, creating an atmosphere of adoration and gratitude. They invite everyone to participate meaningfully, lifting hearts and voices with purpose and joy, and foster a space where worship becomes an authentic response to the divine, glorifying the Lord and drawing closer to Him.

1. *"If you have breath in your lungs today, let it rise as praise to the One who gave it to you!"*
2. *"Let every voice join in praise, for He is worthy of all the breath, all the adoration we can give!"*
3. *"Praise Him, all creation! Every breath we take is a gift, so let's give it back to Him in worship."*
4. *"The breath in our lungs is meant for His glory. Let us use it to declare His greatness!"*
5. *"From the youngest to the oldest, from the mountains to the seas, let everything that has breath praise the Lord!"*

6. *"If the stars could sing, they would join us. Let all creation, all living beings, praise the One who gives life."*
7. *"In every breath we draw, there is a reason to praise. Let us lift our voices to the Giver of Life."*
8. *"From sunrise to sunset, let every moment be filled with praises for the Lord of all."*
9. *"Today, we join all of creation in praise, for His wonders are evident in every living thing."*
10. *"Breathe in His goodness; breathe out His praise. He is the reason for every heartbeat and every breath."*

Song: 1

Verse 1
Let all creation shout and sing,
To You, O Lord, our praises bring.
The rocks cry out, the seas declare,
Your glory fills the earth and air.

Verse 2
The winds and waves resound Your name,
With breath and voice, we do the same.
The creatures join in one accord,
To honor You, our mighty Lord.

Chorus
Let everything that breathes give praise,
Our hearts to You we freely raise.
The earth, the skies, the stars above,
Sing out to You in endless love.

Verse 3
The heavens shout Your majesty,
Your power flows in all we see.
We join the chorus loud and strong,
To You, O Lord, where we belong.

Song: 2

Verse 1
The trees will clap, the hills will sing,
All living things will praises bring.
The rocks cry out, the rivers dance,
In awe of You, there's no chance.

Verse 2
The oceans roar, the winds will shout,
All nature knows what You're about.
Let every breath proclaim Your worth,
For You alone created earth.

Chorus
Let everything with breath sing praise,
In joy and wonder, our voices raise.
To You, O Lord, all glory be,
Forever through eternity.

Verse 3
The birds will soar, the fields will bloom,
In every heart, there's now no room.
For any other name but Yours,
The King of kings, forever endures.

Song: 3

Verse 1
Let every breath bring praise to You,
From fields of green to skies so blue.
The rocks will shout, the trees will sing,
For You, O Lord, are everything.

Verse 2
The rivers flow, the winds will cry,
As all creation lifts You high.
The mountains bow, the valleys call,
In praise of You, who made them all.

Chorus
Let everything with breath sing praise,
To You, O Lord, our hearts we raise.
From earth below to heaven above,
We worship You with endless love.

Verse 3
The birds will chirp, the lions roar,
The seas will crash upon the shore.
Let all creation join in song,
To praise the One who's never wrong.

Song: 4

Verse 1
Let every voice, from low to high,
Join in the chorus of the sky.
The winds will sing, the hills will shout,
Let all creation cry aloud.

Verse 2
The trees will clap, the seas will roar,
The rocks will praise You evermore.
All living things with breath proclaim,
The greatness of Your holy name.

Chorus
Let everything that breathes declare,
The glory of Your love and care.
From earth below to heaven's height,
We praise You, Lord, with all our might.

Verse 3
The birds will sing, the rivers flow,
In all the earth, Your praise will grow.
In every heart and every place,
We lift You up, O God of grace.

Song: 5

Verse 1
Let every breath proclaim Your might,
The rocks cry out both day and night.
The trees, the winds, the oceans roar,
With praises rising evermore.

Verse 2
Let rivers sing and fields rejoice,
All nature lifts a single voice.
From every corner, praise is found,
Your glory echoes all around.

Chorus
Let everything that lives proclaim,
The glory of Your holy name.
With every breath, we lift You high,
And join the praises of the sky.

Verse 3
The flowers bloom to bring You praise,
The sun and moon reflect Your ways.
In all the earth, Your power is seen,
The King of kings, the Lord supreme.

Song: 6

Verse 1
Let everything that breathes proclaim,
The glory of our Savior's name.
From mountain peaks to oceans wide,
We lift His name, the Crucified.

Verse 2
The rocks cry out, the rivers sing,
All praise to Jesus, heaven's King.
The earth responds, the skies declare,
That Jesus reigns beyond compare.

Chorus
Let all creation shout His name,
Let every living thing proclaim.
From every breath and every sound,
Let Jesus' praise be all around.

Verse 3
The winds declare, the flowers bloom,
And all creation leaves the tomb.
In every song, in every cry,
Let Jesus' praise fill earth and sky.

Part 5:
Hebrews 13:15:
A Sacrifice of Praise

Hebrews 13:15:
A Sacrifice of Praise

These exhortations serve as a powerful guide to encourage heartfelt and reverent worship, drawing you into deeper communion with the Lord. By focusing on the relevant them, they remind you of the awe-inspiring character of God and inspire a spirit of reverence.

These words help shift focus from daily distractions to God's greatness and goodness, creating an atmosphere of adoration and gratitude. They invite everyone to participate meaningfully, lifting hearts and voices with purpose and joy, and foster a space where worship becomes an authentic response to the divine, glorifying the Lord and drawing closer to Him.

1. *"Let us offer our praise to Him even when it costs us, for He is worthy of our sacrifice!"*
2. *"Our praises today are an offering, a sacrifice of love and gratitude to our Savior."*
3. *"Even in times of trial, let us offer our hearts in praise, for He is ever faithful."*
4. *"Our praise, no matter the season, is a sweet fragrance rising to the throne of grace."*
5. *"Today, let us bring a sacrifice of praise, surrendering all we are to the One who is worthy."*
6. *"Praise Him in the valleys, praise Him on the mountains—let our lives be a continual offering."*
7. *"Though we may be weary, our praise rises as a sacrifice to the One who sustains us."*

8. *"Let us offer the fruit of our lips, honoring the One who is worthy of all our devotion."*
9. *"Our sacrifice of praise speaks of faith, of love, of surrender. May it rise like incense before Him."*
10. *"In all circumstances, let our praise be our offering, a sacrifice acceptable and pleasing to God."*

Song: 1

Verse 1
With lips that speak, we offer praise,
In every moment, all our days.
Through Christ, we come and glorify,
Your name, O Lord, we lift on high.

Verse 2
A sacrifice we freely bring,
To You, O Lord, our everything.
Through trials, joy, in peace or pain,
Your name forever we proclaim.

Chorus
A sacrifice of praise we give,
For You alone, O Lord, we live.
With open hearts, Your name confess,
Your holy name, we now profess.

Verse 3
The fruit of lips will ever rise,
Our song to You, beyond the skies.
With hearts sincere, our praise resound,
In every place, Your love is found.

Song: 2

Verse 1
Through Jesus now, we bring our praise,
A sacrifice that lasts always.
With lips that speak, with hearts that burn,
To glorify at every turn.

Verse 2
Through every trial, joy, or pain,
We offer praise in Your great name.
Our hearts are Yours, we lift them high,
To honor You, O God Most High.

Chorus
A sacrifice of praise we bring,
To You alone, our glorious King.
With every word, in every breath,
We honor You in life and death.

Verse 3
With open hearts, our voices rise,
To You, O Lord, beyond the skies.
A sacrifice we give each day,
In worship, Lord, we choose to stay

Song: 3

Verse 1
With lips of praise, we come today,
In sacrifice, our hearts we lay.
Through Jesus' blood, we lift our song,
In worship pure, where we belong.

Verse 2
Our offering, O Lord, is clear,
To glorify Your name so dear.
With every breath, our voices soar,
To praise You now and evermore.

Chorus
A sacrifice of praise we bring,
To worship You, our Savior King.
With hearts and lips, we bless Your name,
Forever faithful, still the same.

Verse 3
Through every storm, through joy or pain,
We lift our praise, in loss or gain.
In Jesus' name, we will proclaim,
A sacrifice to lift Your fame.

Song: 4

Verse 1
We bring our praise, a holy gift,
To You, O Lord, our voices lift.
With hearts of thanks, our songs we raise,
In sacrifice of endless praise.

Verse 2
Through Jesus' name, we offer now,
A humble heart, a sacred vow.
Our lips declare Your holy fame,
And bless the power of Your name.

Chorus
A sacrifice of praise we give,
To You, O Lord, in whom we live.
Through every trial, every day,
We lift Your name in endless praise.

Verse 3
With hands held high and hearts of grace,
We bring to You our highest praise.
In every season, through each storm,
Your praise, O Lord, will be our norm.

Song: 5

Verse 1
We bring to You a sacrifice,
Of praise that lifts to paradise.
With hearts and lips, our songs we raise,
In holy awe, we give You praise.

Verse 2
Through Jesus, Lord, our offering,
A sacrifice of praise we bring.
With every word, we bless Your name,
And glorify Your endless fame.

Chorus
A sacrifice of praise we give,
Through You alone, we move and live.
In every trial, in every place,
We worship You, O God of grace.

Verse 3
In good and bad, we bless Your name,
Through every season, still the same.
Our hearts are filled with love and trust,
And in Your presence, Lord, we must.

Song: 6

Verse 1
A sacrifice of praise we give,
Through You, O Christ, we move and live.
In every trial, every gain,
We worship You, the Lamb once slain.

Verse 2
Through Jesus, Lord, our songs ascend,
In every moment, without end.
With open lips, we lift Your name,
Proclaiming now Your endless fame.

Chorus
A sacrifice of praise we bring,
To Jesus Christ, our risen King.
With every breath, with every cry,
We glorify You, Lord Most High.

Verse 3
Through good and bad, we sing Your grace,
With every step, we seek Your face.
Our hearts are Yours, our lives we raise,
In endless songs of Jesus' praise.

Part 6:
John 4:23-24:
Worshipping in Spirit and Truth

John 4:23-24:
Worshipping in Spirit and Truth

These exhortations serve as a powerful guide to encourage heartfelt and reverent worship, drawing you into deeper communion with the Lord. By focusing on the relevant them, they remind you of the awe-inspiring character of God and inspire a spirit of reverence.

These words help shift focus from daily distractions to God's greatness and goodness, creating an atmosphere of adoration and gratitude. They invite everyone to participate meaningfully, lifting hearts and voices with purpose and joy, and foster a space where worship becomes an authentic response to the divine, glorifying the Lord and drawing closer to Him.

1. *"True worshipers, let us come with open hearts and pure spirits, honoring Him in spirit and truth."*
2. *"Today, let's worship from the depths of our hearts, surrendering fully in spirit and in truth."*
3. *"May our worship not just be words, but a true reflection of our hearts, guided by His Spirit."*
4. *"In spirit and in truth, let us lift our praises, desiring to please our holy and loving Father."*
5. *"True worship is not bound by place but by the sincerity of our hearts. Let us worship in spirit and truth!"*
6. *"Today, let us seek His face with honesty and reverence, worshiping Him with our whole being."*

7. *“God is looking for true worshipers. May our worship rise from genuine hearts and open spirits.”*
8. *“In truth and in spirit, let our worship ascend to the One who deserves all we are.”*
9. *“When we worship in spirit and truth, we align our hearts with His, joining heaven’s song.”*
10. *“He desires our true worship. Let us come with hearts humbled and spirits surrendered to Him.”*

Song: 1

Verse 1
In Spirit and in truth we come,
To worship You, O Holy One.
With hearts sincere, with lives laid bare,
We offer praise, beyond compare.

Verse 2
No empty words, no hollow song,
To You alone our praise belongs.
Our spirits bow, our hearts adore,
You are the One we long for more.

Chorus
In Spirit and truth, we worship You,
In every word, in all we do.
Our lives a sacrifice of grace,
To glorify Your holy face.

Verse 3
You seek the ones who worship true,
In Spirit, Lord, we come to You.
With all we are, our voices rise,
To glorify the King of skies.

Song: 2

Verse 1
In Spirit and in truth we come,
Our hearts and lives, before You, One.
No other gods, no idols near,
We worship You with hearts sincere.

Verse 2
In truth we stand, our faith is sure,
To honor You, so true, so pure.
With every word, we lift our song,
To worship where we both belong.

Chorus
In Spirit and truth, we worship You,
With hearts and souls forever true.
No greater joy than this we find,
Than lifting You with all our mind.

Verse 3
You seek the hearts who worship real,
Who long to know and love and feel.
In Spirit, Lord, we seek Your face,
In truth, we rest within Your grace.

Song: 3

Verse 1
In Spirit and in truth we bow,
To worship You in this great hour.
With hearts sincere, we lift our praise,
To honor You through all our days.

Verse 2
No other gods, no idols stand,
We come before You, hand in hand.
In Spirit pure, our hearts will sing,
To glorify our risen King.

Chorus
In Spirit and truth, we worship You,
With all our hearts, forever true.
In every breath, we lift Your name,
Forevermore, You stay the same.

Verse 3
You seek the ones who worship right,
In Spirit, Lord, and truth, so bright.
We give our all, in love and grace,
And seek You, Lord, in every place.

Song: 4

Verse 1
In Spirit true, we come to You,
With hearts sincere, our love renew.
No other god, no idol stands,
But You alone with holy hands.

Verse 2
In truth we worship, Lord, our King,
To honor You in everything.
Our spirits rise, our hearts will soar,
In awe of You forevermore.

Chorus
In Spirit and truth, we seek Your face,
To worship You, our God of grace.
With hearts of fire and lives made new,
We worship only You, Lord true.

Verse 3
You seek the ones whose hearts are pure,
To worship You, forever sure.
In Spirit strong, we lift our voice,
In truth and love, we will rejoice.

Song: 5

Verse 1
In Spirit, Lord, we come to You,
With hearts that seek the pure and true.
We worship now with all our soul,
For You alone make us whole.

Verse 2
In truth, we stand before Your throne,
With hearts and lives that are Your own.
No other god, no other name,
Deserves the glory of Your fame.

Chorus
In Spirit and in truth, we come,
To worship You, the Holy One.
With hearts of fire and lives made new,
We lift our worship up to You.

Verse 3
You seek the ones whose hearts are pure,
To worship You, in love secure.
In Spirit, Lord, our hearts will sing,
In truth, we crown You as our King.

Song: 6

Verse 1
In Spirit, Lord, we worship You,
With hearts that seek Your will so true.
In truth, we bow before Your throne,
In worship, we are not alone.

Verse 2
The Father seeks the ones who stand,
In Spirit, truth, with open hands.
We lift our hearts and minds to You,
In worship pure, in love so true.

Chorus
In Spirit and in truth, we come,
To worship Jesus, Holy One.
With all our hearts, with all our soul,
We praise the One who makes us whole.

Verse 3
In every truth, in every heart,
In worship, Lord, we take our part.
In Spirit, Lord, we sing Your name,
And glorify Your holy fame.

Part 7:
Revelation 5:12:
Worthy is the Lamb Who Was Slain

Revelation 5:12: Worthy is the Lamb Who Was Slain

These exhortations serve as a powerful guide to encourage heartfelt and reverent worship, drawing you into deeper communion with the Lord. By focusing on the relevant them, they remind you of the awe-inspiring character of God and inspire a spirit of reverence.

These words help shift focus from daily distractions to God's greatness and goodness, creating an atmosphere of adoration and gratitude. They invite everyone to participate meaningfully, lifting hearts and voices with purpose and joy, and foster a space where worship becomes an authentic response to the divine, glorifying the Lord and drawing closer to Him.

1. *"He is worthy—the Lamb who was slain for us. Let our voices lift up His name in gratitude and awe."*
2. *"Let us proclaim that the Lamb who took our place is worthy of all honor, glory, and praise."*
3. *"Jesus, the Lamb, our Redeemer, is worthy of all we have. Let us pour out our love upon Him."*
4. *"Worthy is the Lamb! With all creation, we declare His power, glory, and majesty."*
5. *"The Lamb who was slain is worthy of every song we sing, every breath we breathe, and every prayer we utter."*
6. *"Let us honor the Lamb, who sacrificed all for us, with praises that resound throughout eternity."*

7. *“Worthy is the Lamb, for He bore our sins. Let our hearts overflow with worship.”*
8. *“Today, we join the saints in declaring that He alone is worthy—the Lamb who reigns forever.”*
9. *“In awe, we lift up the name of Jesus, the Lamb, who is worthy of all honor and blessing.”*
10. *“To the Lamb who was slain, we give all praise, for He alone is worthy to be exalted.”*

Song: 1

Verse 1
Worthy is the Lamb who died,
Who rose again, now glorified.
To Him be power, strength, and praise,
We lift our voices all our days.

Verse 2
In heaven's courts, the song resounds,
As angels bow on holy grounds.
All creatures sing, both great and small,
To Him who reigns, the Lord of all.

Chorus
Worthy is the Lamb who died,
Exalted now and glorified.
To Him, all honor and all fame,
We lift the power of His name.

Verse 3
The saints and angels join the song,
With voices loud, both pure and strong.
All praise belongs to Christ alone,
To Him we bring our highest tone.

Song: 2

Verse 1
Worthy is the Lamb once slain,
Who conquered death, who broke the chain.
To Him belongs all power and might,
Our risen Lord, our guiding light.

Verse 2
With heaven's host, we lift Your name,
And cry, "Worthy!" with no shame.
The Lamb who died, yet rose again,
Forevermore, He will reign.

Chorus
Worthy is the Lamb who died,
Exalted now, He's glorified.
All honor, praise, and glory sing,
To Jesus Christ, our risen King.

Verse 3
The saints and angels join the sound,
With worship rising all around.
To Christ the Lamb, our hearts we bring,
In endless song, to Him we sing.

Song: 3

Verse 1
Worthy is the Lamb, holy and bright,
Who reigns in glory, power, and might.
To You, all honor, endless praise,
In reverent awe, our voices raise.

Verse 2
The heavens sing of mercy's crown,
For sin You bore, You laid it down.
Oh, spotless Lamb, Your grace abounds,
In sacred love, my heart resounds.

Chorus
Worthy, worthy, Lamb of grace,
Forever ruling time and space.
Our song shall rise, our hearts proclaim,
Glory to Your holy name.

Verse 3
Before the throne, with voices pure,
Your love endures, steadfast and sure.
Redeemer, Savior, Prince of Peace,
All songs to You shall never cease.

Song: 4

Verse 1
In robes of white, You stand above,
Crowned with power and endless love.
Our voices rise to lift Your fame,
For only You deserve our claim.

Verse 2
For all who trust, You broke the chains,
Worthy Lamb, who bore our pains.
In faith and awe, our praises flow,
For love that only You bestow.

Chorus
All honor, glory, majesty,
To You, the Lamb who set us free.
In worship pure, our hearts belong,
To You, our everlasting song.

Verse 3
Though skies may fade, and stars grow dim,
Our songs will rise forever to Him.
Eternal King, who was and is,
Our worthy Lamb, forever His.

Song: 5

Verse 1
Lamb of God, exalted high,
Your boundless love, we magnify.
Forever crowned, in robes of light,
You conquered death with holy might.

Verse 2
From throne above, Your voice declares,
Mercy flows and grace repairs.
We lift our praise, our hearts aligned,
In worship true, Your worth defined.

Chorus
Eternal Worth, You wear the crown,
Our hearts in awe are kneeling down.
No other name could rise above,
The Lamb enthroned in endless love.

Verse 3
In heavenly courts, our voices blend,
In worship that shall never end.
For every soul You've freed and won,
Worthy Lamb, God's only Son.

Song: 6

Verse 1
Holy Lamb, who wore our shame,
We lift You high, we praise Your name.
Your blood has washed our sins away,
In grateful song, we humbly pray.

Verse 2
With angels, saints, our voices meet,
Around Your throne, at mercy's seat.
We crown You now, our souls take flight,
In worship full, You are our Light.

Chorus
Be glorified, O Lamb of grace,
In every heart, in every place.
Our praise ascends like heaven’s fire,
To worship You, our soul’s desire.

Verse 3
In endless songs, our spirits soar,
To praise the Lamb we both adore.
From earth to skies, let voices ring,
For Christ our Lord, our risen King.

Part 8:
1 Chronicles 16:29: Worshipping Jesus in the Splendor of Holiness

1 Chronicles 16:29: Worshipping Jesus in the Splendor of Holiness

These exhortations serve as a powerful guide to encourage heartfelt and reverent worship, drawing you into deeper communion with the Lord. By focusing on the relevant them, they remind you of the awe-inspiring character of God and inspire a spirit of reverence.

These words help shift focus from daily distractions to God's greatness and goodness, creating an atmosphere of adoration and gratitude. They invite everyone to participate meaningfully, lifting hearts and voices with purpose and joy, and foster a space where worship becomes an authentic response to the divine, glorifying the Lord and drawing closer to Him.

1. *"Let us enter His presence in reverence, worshiping Him in the beauty and splendor of His holiness."*
2. *"Today, let's stand in awe of His holy presence, worshiping Him with pure and undivided hearts."*
3. *"We bow before His holiness, acknowledging His majesty and honoring Him with all that we are."*
4. *"With reverence, let us approach Him, clothed in humility, as we honor His holy name."*
5. *"Worship Him in the splendor of holiness, for there is none like our holy and righteous King!"*
6. *"Our God is holy. Let our worship reflect His beauty and the splendor of His glory."*

7. *“In awe and reverence, let us come before our holy God, honoring Him with hearts full of worship.”*
8. *“He is clothed in majesty and splendor. Let our worship rise in reverence for His holiness.”*
9. *“Let us worship Jesus with pure hearts, for He is holy and worthy of all our adoration.”*
10. *“In His holy presence, let our worship be a reflection of His splendor and majesty.”*

Song: 1

Verse 1
In holiness, we bow and sing,
To You, O Christ, our risen King.
We bring our offering to Your throne,
And worship You, and You alone.

Verse 2
Ascribe to Christ the glory due,
In splendor, Lord, we worship You.
Your holiness is pure and bright,
And in Your love, we find delight.

Chorus
Worship Christ in holiness,
Our songs of praise, we now confess.
In splendor, Lord, we lift Your name,
Forever glorified the same.

Verse 3
Before Your throne, we humbly stand,
With hearts and lives in Your command.
In holiness, O Lord, we bow,
To worship You, forever now.

Song: 2

Verse 1
In splendor bright, You reign above,
Cloaked in holiness and love.
Majesty and grace surround,
In awe and wonder, we are found.

Verse 2
You hold the stars, the heavens' light,
Holy One, forever bright.
With hearts and hands, to You we sing,
The glorious splendor of our King.

Chorus
Holy, holy, Lord of all,
To You alone, our praises call.
We worship in Your righteousness,
Adoring You, in holiness.

Verse 3
No other name so pure, so true,
In awe and fear, we come to You.
You wear the crown, unmatched and high,
In splendor bright, You glorify.

Song: 3

Verse 1
Clothed in might, robed in light,
You are holy, pure, and bright.
In all Your splendor, Lord, we gaze,
Our hearts pour out in endless praise.

Verse 2
In beauty's grace, in mercy's hand,
The holy King of all the land.
We bow before Your throne so grand,
For You alone our hearts will stand.

Chorus
Majesty, we lift You high,
Holy Lord, the Great Most High.
In splendor pure and righteousness,
We worship You, O Holiness.

Verse 3
O King of Kings, our praise ascends,
To You, our worship never ends.
In sacred awe, we lift Your name,
With hearts of fire, we proclaim.

Song: 4

Verse 1
O holy King in robes of light,
In Your splendor, pure and bright.
We lift our voice, our spirits sing,
For You alone, eternal King.

Verse 2
With hands raised high and hearts laid bare,
In reverent awe, we come in prayer.
You shine with beauty none can claim,
All glory given to Your name.

Chorus
Pure and holy, Lamb adored,
You reign forever, Sovereign Lord.
In beauty's grace, we worship now,
Before Your throne, in awe we bow.

\Verse 3
From dawn to dusk, our praise shall ring,
In every heart, our Savior King.
Majestic God, forever reign,
Our songs declare Your holy name.

Song: 5

Verse 1
In sacred light, You shine so clear,
Our Holy God, we draw near.
Your glory fills the earth and sky,
Our voices lift, our praises fly.

Verse 2
Adorned in robes of purest white,
Majestic King, our heart's delight.
To You, we bring our songs of love,
To honor You, O Lord above.

Chorus
Holy, holy, Lord of Grace,
We worship You in this holy place.
In splendor bright, our praises rise,
To You alone, the Lord most high.

Verse 3
In holy fear, in reverent awe,
We bow before Your sacred law.
With every breath, Your name we bless,
Our worship clothed in holiness.

Song: 6

Verse 1
In the splendor of Your holiness, we bow,
Our hearts surrendered, in awe we stand now.
You reign in glory, forever the same,
We lift up praises to Your holy name.

Verse 2
Your light surrounds us, pure and bright,
Guiding us onward, through each day and night.
Majestic and holy, all goodness You bring,
Our voices rise high as Your praises we sing.

Chorus
Glory and honor, to You we sing,
Holy and mighty, our Savior, our King.
All creation echoes, Your majesty grand,
In the splendor of holiness, we firmly stand.

Verse 3
From depths of our soul, our worship we give,
In reverence and awe, for You we live.
To the King eternal, to You alone,
Our songs of worship before Your throne.

Part 9:
Isaiah 12:5-6:
Singing to Jesus for His Glorious Works

Isaiah 12:5-6: Singing to Jesus for His Glorious Works

These exhortations serve as a powerful guide to encourage heartfelt and reverent worship, drawing you into deeper communion with the Lord. By focusing on the relevant them, they remind you of the awe-inspiring character of God and inspire a spirit of reverence.

These words help shift focus from daily distractions to God's greatness and goodness, creating an atmosphere of adoration and gratitude. They invite everyone to participate meaningfully, lifting hearts and voices with purpose and joy, and foster a space where worship becomes an authentic response to the divine, glorifying the Lord and drawing closer to Him.

1. *"Let us sing joyfully to the Lord for His mighty deeds and wondrous works in our lives!"*
2. *"Today, we lift our voices, celebrating the glorious works of our Savior who reigns with power and grace."*
3. *"Let's declare His marvelous deeds, singing with hearts full of gratitude for His endless mercy."*
4. *"The Lord has done great things! Let our song be filled with joy for His goodness and grace."*
5. *"Sing praises to our King, for His love endures forever and His works are mighty and glorious."*
6. *"With joyful hearts, let us celebrate the glorious works of Jesus, our Redeemer and King."*

7. *“Our God has done great things! Let us sing and rejoice for His works are wondrous and true.”*
8. *“Join in song, for our God is worthy of praise for all He has done and all He will do.”*
9. *“Lift your voice in worship, thanking Him for His goodness, faithfulness, and mighty deeds!”*
10. *“Let us sing with all that we have, for our Savior’s works are great, and His love is eternal.”*

Song: 1

Verse 1
Sing to the Lord for all He's done,
Our Savior, Christ, God's only Son.
With joy, we shout His wondrous name,
And tell the world of His great fame.

Verse 2
For Jesus, Lord, has done great things,
And in His name, salvation rings.
In every land, let praises rise,
To glorify the Lord Most High.

Chorus
We sing to You, O Christ, our King,
For You have done great everything.
In every heart, in every tongue,
Your wondrous works are ever sung.

Verse 3
Shout for joy, O people bright,
For Jesus shines as morning light.
The world will know His power and grace,
In every time, in every place.

Song: 2

Verse 1
Your mighty works, we sing and shout,
In every land, we spread about.
With joy, we tell what You have done,
O Savior King, the Righteous One.

Verse 2
From dawn's first light to stars above,
We lift our songs of endless love.
Your wonders fill the earth and sky,
To You alone, our praises fly.

Chorus
Marvelous deeds, O glorious King,
To You alone, our hearts will sing.
In every place, Your name we raise,
Our voices lifted high in praise.

Verse 3
With grateful hearts, Your works we share,
Declaring loud, Your love and care.
Our songs of joy, we bring to You,
For all the mighty things You do.

Song: 3

Verse 1
You've healed the broken, set us free,
Our hearts rejoice in victory.
We sing of love that knows no end,
Our Savior, King, and dearest Friend.

Verse 2
Your works are great, Your love profound,
With joyous songs, we make our sound.
In every breath, Your praise we sing,
For You alone, our risen King.

Chorus
Glory to Your holy name,
Forevermore we'll sing Your fame.
For all You've done, our hearts will soar,
To praise You, Lord, forevermore.

Verse 3
In every trial, You bring us through,
Our steadfast trust remains in You.
With songs of joy, our hearts proclaim,
The wonders of Your holy name.

Song: 4

Verse 1
With songs of joy, we shout Your praise,
Our hearts are set on endless days.
Your works are mighty, true, and grand,
We lift Your name in every land.

Verse 2
In times of joy, in darkest night,
Your hand has led us by Your light.
We sing of love, so strong and pure,
In You alone, our hearts are sure.

Chorus
Forever praises to Your name,
Our mighty Lord, unchanging flame.
For all You are, for all You've done,
We lift our songs to Christ the Son.

Verse 3
Your wonders tell of love divine,
Your works declare Your holy sign.
O faithful God, we sing anew,
Our endless praise, O Lord, to You.

Song: 5

Verse 1
We stand in awe of all You've done,
O Holy God, the Risen One.
Your power reigns in earth and sky,
To You, O Lord, we lift our cry.

Verse 2
Your hands have shaped the mountains high,
Your voice commands both sea and sky.
In awe, we sing of love so true,
Our mighty King, we worship You.

Chorus
Mighty works and holy praise,
To You alone our voices raise.
In every tongue, Your name we sing,
To honor You, our sovereign King.

Verse 3
With hearts of joy, our songs arise,
To praise the One who never dies.
Forever Lord, Your name we bless,
Our songs declare Your righteousness.

Song: 6

Verse 1
With joyful hearts, we come and sing,
For every gift and wondrous thing.
You heal, restore, and make us whole,
O mighty Lord of every soul.

Verse 2
Your works are great, Your love is sure,
Your mercy stands forever pure.
In songs of praise, we lift Your name,
Declaring loud, Your holy fame.

Chorus
In awe of Your deeds, O Lord we stand,
With songs of joy in every land.
Forevermore, Your name we raise,
In endless love, in endless praise.

Verse 3
From sea to sky, Your works abound,
Your glory fills the earth around.
With grateful hearts, we sing to You,
Our Savior, faithful, pure, and true.

Conclusion

As you come to the end of this collection of songs, remember that worship is not confined to the lyrics or melodies you create—it's a living, breathing expression of your heart to God.
These 40 songs are merely starting points for a deeper, personal journey into His presence. Whether you sing them alone in the quiet of your home or with others in joyous celebration, know that every note, every word, and every moment of worship is precious to the Lord.
You have the freedom to shape these songs in your own way, reflecting your unique relationship with God and Jesus Christ. Let these songs inspire you to worship Him daily, offering melodies that rise from your spirit. As you continue to seek Him through your own tunes, harmonies, and expressions of praise, may you encounter the Almighty in powerful and personal ways.

Worship boldly, sing freely, and let your heart overflow with adoration for our great God and Savior, Jesus Christ.

About the Author
'GERARD ASSEY'

Gerard Assey is a Graduate in Economics, a PGD in Management (HRD) and holds a Doctorate in Leadership. Gerard holds several International Qualifications in Sales, Debt Collection, Training & Teaching, and is a 'Fellow' of the prestigious 'Institute of Sales & Marketing Management'-UK, a Certified NLP Practitioner, a 'Certified Trainer', an 'Accredited Management Teacher-Behavioral Sciences', a 'Certified Competency Facilitator', a 'Certified Management Consultant'- (the International credentials of a professional management consultant, awarded in accordance with global standards of the ICMCI); and a Certification from the University of Michigan in 'Successful Negotiation: Essential Strategies and Skills'

He is also a Member of the 'National Association of Sales Professionals' backed with several years experience in varied industries, both in India and Overseas. He also holds an 'Etiquette Consultant' Certification from the USA (by Sue Fox, Author of Best Seller: 'Business Etiquette for Dummies'. She has trained some of the top celebrities' world over). He was also a recipient of a scholarship for extensive training in Japan on 'Corporate Management for India'.

Gerard Assey is 'Founder & Chief Corporate Trainer' of the Group: '**Citius, Altius, Fortius Unlimited**'- an organization that **celebrated 20 years of Glorious Service** in 2021, focusing on 3 Core Competencies:

People. Performance. Profit; in functional areas of Sales & Marketing, HR & Organizational Development, covering Recruitment, Training & Consultancy!

Having managed organizations with large Sales Forces in India & Overseas, his specialization cover extensive areas of Sales Training (All levels - Presentation, Negotiation, Key/ Strategic Accounts Management & Managerial Skills for all sectors), Bid Proposal/ Capture Planning/ Management Trainings, Retail Sales, Customer Service & Customer Retention Programs, Training for Prevention & Collection of Debt, Self & Personal Development Programs (Time Management, Teamwork & Team Building, Business Etiquette & Personal Grooming, Leadership & Managerial Skills, People Management Skills, Train-the-Trainer etc), including preparation of Custom-designed Business Manuals for Internal (HR, Induction, and Sales etc) & External use (Instruction, User Manuals).

Gerard has successfully conducted over 6200 Trainings & Workshops (as of June '24) all across India, Middle East, Africa, Europe & S.E. Asia. Besides public programs conducted regularly, both in India & Overseas, he has some of the top names as clients whom he services from Single Owners to large Public & Government undertakings, covering all sectors, for their in-house needs.

His website: www.CollectionSkills.com is the only one in this part of the world to be featured in the 'Collections & Credit Risk Magazine-USA' under 'Who's Who in Training' and ranks TOP, along with other websites listed below on most search engines.

Gerard is author of 157 books already (Oct 2024), all the books being available on all online platforms and outlets as E-books and Paperbacks

A few of our business related books:

1. Bite-sized Bits on Commonsense Management
2. Heart to Heart on Life's Principles'
3. How to become a Successful Manager
4. The Sales Professionals' Master Workbook of S.Y.S.T.E.M.S
5. The Professional Business Email Etiquette Handbook & Guide
6. The Professional Business Video-Conferencing Etiquette Handbook & Guide
7. Professional Presentation Skills
8. Exceptional Customer Service
9. Professional Tele-Marketing Skills
10. Professional Debt Collection Skills
11. The G.R.E.A.T. Sales & Service Workbook
12. Sales Training Advantage for Results (*The Ultimate Sales Training Manual to enable you stand out as a S.T.A.R.*)
13. CEO Daily Planner & Organizer
14. The Sales Professionals' Master Daily Planner
15. The Professional Debt Collector's Master Daily Planner
16. My Daily Planner & Organizer
17. MY EMERGENCY INFORMATION RECORD (Family Emergency & Peace of Mind Planner)
18. The Ultimate Therapist & Counselors Planner and Organizer
19. Building an Ethical Workplace
20. Managing Relationships at Work
21. Managing Business Meetings Effectively
22. Effective Delegation Skills
23. Goal Setting for Success
24. B2B Selling by Email
25. Professional Business Etiquette & Grooming
26. Dining Etiquette & Table Manners
27. Effective Networking Skills
28. Grooming, Etiquette & Manners for Teens, Young Adults & Future Leaders
29. Inter-Personal Skills
30. Get Ready, Get Hired!
31. Selling in a Recession

32. Effective Receivables Management in an Economic Downturn!
33. Real Estate & Property Sales Training
34. Credit Sales & Accounts Receivable Management
35. Selling Skills for Real Estate & Property Advisors
36. Take G.R.E.A.T. C.A.R.E!
37. Spa, Salon & Health Club Selling Skills
38. Selling Travel, Holiday & MICE Services
39. Selling Skills for Spa's, Salons & Health Clubs
40. Retailing in Salons & Spas
41. Selling Holiday, Vacation, Tours & Packages
42. The Power of Sales Referrals
43. Selling Luxury
44. Technical Selling Skills
45. Financial Advisors Sales Training
46. Dealing with Burnout at Work Monopolize Your Markets
47. Selling to Affluent Customers
48. Growing up with Grace
49. Financial Selling Skills
50. *The Effective Manager's Guide: Key Skills to Thrive*
51. From Aspiring to Inspiring: A Guide for New Managers on the Rise
52. The Power of Focus
53. Selling with Integrity: Sell Like Jesus The Perfect Role Model!
54. 31 Habits of Champions: Your 31-Day Journey to Greatness
55. Rejecting Grasshopper Talk: From Grasshopper to Giant-Killer-*Defeating Giants Daily!*
56. Navigate the AI-Powered Future of Bid & Proposals: Up-Skill to Stay Relevant with Alternative Career Paths & Opportunities
57. Hiring Sales Winners
58. Present with Impact
59. Success Unlocked: *Breaking Free from Habits that Hold You Back*
60. Complaints to Cheers, Feedback to Gold: Mastering Complaints Management
61. Thriving Together: *Cultivating Diversity, Equity, and Inclusion*
62. Coaching Skills for Sales Managers

63. Soaring to Success in Business & Leadership: Swifter, Higher, Stronger!
64. From Classroom to Podium: A Student's Guide to Powerful Public Speaking & Presentation Skills
65. Developing Self-Discipline
66. The CEO's 31-Day Power Plan: Unlocking Success through Essential Traits
67. Credibility Matters
68. A Winning Attitude
69. Bid & Proposal Management Using AI
70. Sales Forecasting: A Practical & Proven Guide to Strategic Sales Forecasting
71. Elevate & Energize: *50 Dynamic & Fun Activities for Peak Workplace Morale*
72. 'Sales SOS! Sales on Fire! *30 Days to Conquer Chaos & the Nightmares of Success!'*
73. Mastering Sales Managerial Skills: *Building High-Performing Teams & Driving Exceptional Results*
74. Eagle-Eyed Leadership: Unleashing the Power of 31 Lessons from Eagles
75. The Ultimate Employee Training Guide: *Training Today, Leading Tomorrow*
76. Being More Accountable at Work
77. Creating a Culture of Continuous Improvement
78. Effective Questioning & Listening Skills
79. The Power of Value Selling
80. The Growth Mindset
81. Mastering Professional Help Desk Skills
82. The Power to Lead with Empathy
83. Being Prepared: The Key to Unlocking Success
84. Youthful Spark-Youth Energizers, Activities and Games-Igniting the Fun in Youth
85. Ignite your Motivation for Success
86. Elevate Your Executive Presence: *Your Roadmap to Executive Excellence*
87. Smart Decisions: *Mastering Problem Solving with Strategic Solutions for Business Success*
88. Strategic Planning: *Developing and Implementing Strategic Plans to Achieve Long-Term Business Goals*
89. The Power of Stay Interviews
90. Developing G.R.I.T.
91. Adaptability

92. Diagnosis- *A Key Skill for Leadership*
93. The Burnout-Proof Salesperson: *The Master Guide to Preventing Stress & Burnout*- Strategies for Thriving in Sales
94. Learning from Failure: *Keys to Success*
95. Customer Success Management
96. Overcoming the Killers of Motivation
97. The C-Suite Code: *Mastering Skills for Executive Excellence'*
98. Dealing with Difficult Customers
99. Unlocking Your Potential: Mastering the Top 20 Life Skills for a Brighter Future
100. Nurturing Tomorrow's Leaders: *Essential Soft Skills Every Child Must Learn*
101. Lively & Fun Party Games for Seniors & Elders
102. Role Playing for Sales Champions: From Practice to Performance
103. Fun and Exciting Party Games for Kids
104. Case Studies for Sales
105. Role-Playing for Unbeatable Customer Service
106. Case Studies in Customer Service
107. Case Studies in Winning Negotiations
108. Case Studies in Management & Leadership
109. Case Studies in Human Resources & Talent Management
110. CEO Success Blueprint: The Essential Toolkit for CEOs and C-Level Executives
111. The Salesperson's Self-Coaching Guide: *Master Your Own Self-Coaching Plan for Success*
112. Overcoming Procrastination: *Your Ultimate Guide to Stop Delaying and Start Living Your Best Life*

From the Ministry side, Gerard graduated in the very first batch of Charis Bible College-India & had for over 9 years served as a Part-time Faculty at Charis Bible College-Chennai (Andrew Wommack Ministries-Colorado, USA).
He is also a graduate of the Advanced Mentorship Program (AMP) and the Circle Of Ministerial Engagement (C.O.M.E.) of Prophet Jerome Fernando and a Spiritual Son of the Esteemed Prophet.
An accomplished author of several Secular & Christian Books, Gerard has been on the board of a few

international organizations and boasts of being the SON of the MOST HIGH GOD: An ordinary guy following an extraordinary GOD!

...And some of his most recent Christian Books being:

1. A Bouquet of Praises for My KING
2. Christian Jokes for the Serious Religious' Folks!
3. Jesus Healed You!
4. Praise24Ever! (also in Tamil version)
5. The 5G Network of GOD
6. Building Faith over F.E.A.R- FACE EVERYTHING AND RISE with JESUS
7. Hebrew and Greek Praise and Worship Words
8. Godly Mothers' and Grandmothers' Bible Story time for Kids!
9. Miracles of Jesus in Pictures
10. Raise your Praise all 365 Days
11. Thanking GOD with an Attitude of Gratitude
12. Meditating on the Attributes of GOD
13. Puppet Scripts
14. Alcohol Ruins, JESUS Reforms, Renews & Restores!
15. Habakkuk 2:2 Christian Daily Journal, Planner & Organizer
16. ABC of GOD's Word for Handwriting Practice
17. Daily Bible Verse Handwriting Practice (Building Godly Character & Faith through Cursive Handwriting Practice!)
18. Guiding Light: Fun & Faith-Building Bible Activities for Children
19. Rejecting Grasshopper Talk: From Grasshopper to Giant-Killer-*Defeating Giants Daily!*
20. Teen Titans of Faith: *Building Courage, Determination & Christ-like-Esteem*
21. I AM Empowered: *Unleashing Divine Power with Positive Declarations*
22. Be A Solution Provider-*From Passion to Purpose*: *A Biblical Guide to Being the Answer to the World!*
23. Miracles of JESUS
24. Parables of Jesus for a Meaningful Life!
25. A Grateful Heart: Importance of Sharing Testimonies of GOD's Grace
26. Melodies of Worship to JESUS: 31 Songs of Praise & Worship From My Heart to HIS!

27. I AM SO BLESSED!
28. My Daily Cup of Energizer
29. 31 Leadership Lessons *from* Jesus- *The Supreme Leader*
30. Peace Amidst Storms: A Biblical Guide to Conquering S.T.R.E.S.S.
31. Rise Above: 20 Biblical Eagle Lessons for Life's Triumphs
32. Godly Goal Setting: *The FAITHFUL Blueprint for a Purpose-Driven Life*
33. The Profound Attributes of our Mighty GOD: Understanding the 10S's of the Almighty
34. Worship Now, Worship Forever: *A Journey from Earthly Praise to Eternal Glory*

Besides regularly contributing to business & trade journals, including international ones such as the 'Creative Training Techniques' and the 'Sales News' of the U.S.A, He is also a member of several prestigious bodies & trade associations, having participated in many Conferences & Workshops in India & Overseas.

Prior to his last assignment of leading & managing a large MNC as head, Gerard had a 3-year stint in the Middle East as a Consultant with a leading British Consultancy Firm.

As the past 'Official Country Representative' for the International Business Award- 'THE STEVIES'-(the business world's own Oscar) for about 4 years- he ensured a few Indian companies that qualify for the same every year!

Gerard can be contacted at:
Email: training@Sales-Training.in,training@CollectionSkills.com
Websites:
www.Sales-Training.in
www.EtiquetteWorks.in
www.CollectionSkills.com
www.RetailSalesTraining.in
www.SalesTrainingIndia.com
www.ManualPreparation.com
www.TrainingWithPuppets.com
www.FirstContactAcademy.com
www.SalesAndMarketingRecruiter.com

Our TRAININGS that can help your team

- ✓ **Sales Effectiveness**: Selling Skills for any Sector: Service/ Logistics/ FMCG Realty/ Insurance & Finance/ Media/ SPA's, Health Clubs & Salons/ Key Account Management, Effective Negotiation Skills/ Bid & Proposal Management Skills/ Retail Sales Training: Any Sector (Auto, Jewelry, Clothing, Luxury etc)
- ✓ **Customer Service Skills**-Complaints Handling & Customer Retention
- ✓ **Debt Prevention & Collection Skills**
- ✓ **Etiquette & Grooming**
- ✓ **Leadership & Managerial Skills**
- ✓ **Self & Personal Development Skills**: Presentation Skills/ Effective Communication Skills/Business Proposal Writing Skills/ Problem Solving & Decision Making Skills/ Empowering Secretaries-The perfect PA! (For Secretaries & PA's)/ Effective Time Management/ Teamwork & Teambuilding/ P.R.I.D.E- **P**ersonal **R**esponsibility **I**n **D**elivering **E**xcellence

www.ingramcontent.com/pod-product-compliance
Lightning Source LLC
LaVergne TN
LVHW010114170826
845678LV00012B/2407
* 9 7 8 8 1 9 7 9 6 5 4 4 9 *